Date Due

MAR 1 7 1997		
APR 1 0 1997		
MAR 1 8 1998		
OCT 2 2 1999		
SEP 2 9 2000		
APR 0 6 2002		
OCT 0 4 2004		

BRODART, CO.   Cat. No. 23-233-003   Printed in U.S.A.

THE PUEBLOS

SUZANNE POWELL

THE PUEBLOS

Franklin Watts   New York   Chicago   London   Sydney   A First Book

Cover photograph copyright ©: Jerry Jacka
Map by Joe LeMonnier

Photographs copyright ©: Stephen Trimble: 3, 19, 40 (top and bottom),
43, 44 (bottom) 53, 58; John Running: 12, 17, 22, 25, 27 (bottom), 37,
44 (top), 47, 50 (bottom), 52; North Wind Picture Archives: 27 (top),
29, 56; Jerry Jacka: 33; Tom Till/Tony Stone Images: 35; T. Harmon
Parkhurst, Museum of New Mexico: 50 (top)

Library of Congress Cataloging in Publication Data
Powell, Suzanne I.
The Pueblos / by Suzanne Powell.
p. cm. — (A First book)
Includes bibliographical references (p.) and index.
Summary: Discusses the traditional and modern way of life of the Pueblos,
examining their history, culture, religion, and ability to survive and thrive
in difficult conditions.
ISBN 0-531-20068-X (lib. bdg.)—ISBN 0-531-15703-2 (pbk.)
1. Pueblo Indians—Juvenile literature. [1. Pueblo Indians. 2. Indians of
North America—Southwest, New.] I. Title. II. Series
E99.P9P686   1993
978.9'004974-dc20   93-18368 CIP AC

CONTENTS

DEDICATION TO PUEBLO INDIANS

Day is done.
Nightfall is slowly approaching.
The evening sun casts its
multicolored lights
from the western sky.

Hues of reds, pinks, purples
and blues spotlight
the most artful works of
Mother Nature.

There, camouflaged in
a high cliffwall,
so masterfully constructed,
a village.

The majestic mountains
offer the perfect background
to this awesome sight.

The movement of tiny beings so high up would
catch the eye of the most
unassuming visitor.

Living in a world so high
above the rest, with no visible
means of entrance.

A society of people, with
strong religious convictions
bond as one with nature
to live a truly peaceful life.

From these before us,
we learn.

—Suzanne Powell

To Ben, Eric, and David —
my daily inspirations.

To all children —
may you learn to accept and respect
those who came before you.

THE PUEBLO

INTRODUCTION

Through the work and studies of anthropologists and archaeologists, it is believed the first peoples came to the Americas from Asia at least 20,000 years ago. Coming by way of Alaska and working their way south, they began to settle in what is now Canada and the United States.

Not much is known about these early peoples. Books were not written because there wasn't a written language. Most of what we do know comes from the objects they used and left behind.

Different groups came and settled in different areas of North America. Some settled where there was plenty of game and became hunters. Others sought out areas around lakes, rivers, or the sea coast to fish. The people who settled in the pueblos discovered maize, better known to us as corn, and became farmers.

THESE ANASAZI RUINS ARE PRESERVED AT THE WUPATKI
NATIONAL MONUMENT SITE IN NORTHEASTERN ARIZONA.

HISTORY

Around the year 400 A.D., more than 1,500 years ago, there existed a group of people known as the Anasazi, meaning "ancient ones." These peaceful people lived in the country of red-rock canyons and sagebrush flats, which we recognize today as northeastern Arizona, northwestern New Mexico, and parts of Utah and Colorado. The Anasazi were called "basket-makers," because their baskets were so tightly woven together that they were used to carry water.

The dead of the Anasazi were often buried in storage pits. During the burial rite, surviving relatives would place weapons, ornaments, and food with the bodies. The deceased were then carefully wrapped up in mats or animal skins, and their heads were covered with a basket.

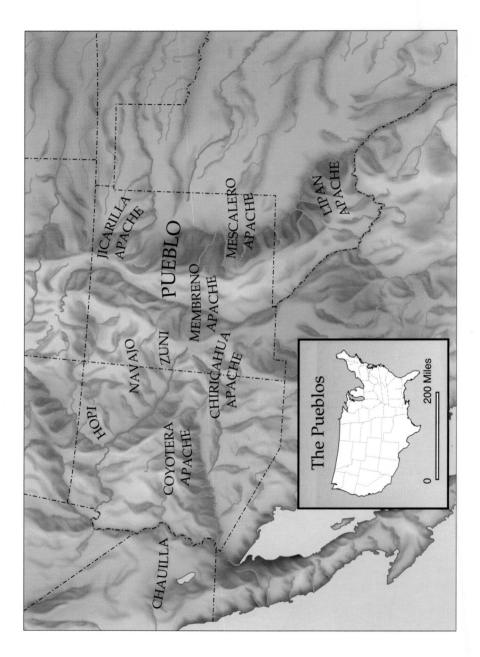

The Pueblos

200 Miles

0

JICARILLA APACHE

PUEBLO

MESCALERO APACHE

LIPAN APACHE

MEMBRENO APACHE

ZUNI

NAVAJO

CHIRICAHUA APACHE

HOPI

COYOTERA APACHE

CHAUILLA

The descendants of the Anasazi people were called "Pueblos" by the Spanish. Pueblo means village or town in Spanish. Spaniards used the name "Pueblo" to refer to both the people and their villages.

The first Europeans to see these Indians were the Spaniards. These Spanish explorers arrived in the southwest part of our country sixty-six years before the Pilgrims arrived at Plymouth Rock.

In 1598, the Spaniards developed a settlement near a Pueblo village. They forced the Pueblos to work for them and turn over some of their crops. As forced laborers, the Pueblos worked for the Spaniards in mines and on ranches. They were also made to follow the Roman Catholic ways instead of their own religious beliefs. Not understanding these Indians' religious and social practices, the Spaniards insisted that each pueblo, or village, should have a governor, so the Indians were forced to elect governors.

Between 1645 and 1680, the Indians rebelled against cruel, forced labor. Finally joining forces with the Hopis and Apaches, the Pueblos set out to fight the Spaniards. Knotted cords were sent to all tribes by messengers, indicating the day the rebellion would take place. The Spaniards learned of their plan, and when the Indians found they had been discovered they started the rebellion two days in advance.

During the rebellion, hundreds of Spaniards were killed. The Indians destroyed many written records, as well as churches and missions belonging to the Spaniards. The surviving Spaniards fled this area of the country, returning twelve years later to regain control of the Indians. By the early 1700s, the Spaniards ruled over all the Pueblo tribes of the Rio Grande region.

The Spaniards put many Pueblos into forced labor, and altered their society in many ways. The Pueblos had only dogs and turkeys, but the Spanish brought them sheep, goats, cows, oxen, horses, mules, chickens, and pigs. These animals proved useful as livestock and beasts of burden, but the grazing animals often invaded the Pueblos' cornfields.

The Spaniards also introduced the Indians to such European crops as apples, peaches, pears, medicinal herbs, onions, cabbages, and chick peas, as well as chilies and tomatoes from Mexico. In return, the Pueblos shared their dry farming techniques with the Spaniards.

For generations, the Indians had been using stone masonry walls to build their dwellings. The Spanish brought the idea of adobe-brick, corner fireplaces, and chimneys.

THIS PICTOGRAPH FROM CANYON DE CHELLY NATIONAL
MONUMENT IN NORTHEASTERN ARIZONA DEPICTS THE SPANISH
CONQUEST OF THE PUEBLO INDIANS.

THE SOUTHWEST

The Pueblo Indians settled in the southwestern part of the United States. Their pueblos or villages were found in areas of five different states: Arizona, Nevada, New Mexico, Utah, and Colorado. Some of the land was hot, dry desert, separated by rocky cliffs, multicolored mesas, and deep canyons. Snowcapped mountains could be seen in the distance. A multitude of nature's finest works were blended in harmony, but created what would seem a forbidding place for people to live. Harsh climatic conditions such as droughts, high winds, sandstorms, flash floods, and blizzards offered the Pueblos their biggest challenge of survival.

ACOMA PUEBLO, WEST OF ALBUQUERQUE, NEW MEXICO,
SITS AMID THE DRAMATIC AND STARK TERRAIN OF
THE AMERICAN SOUTHWEST.

Most of the land was rocky, with a sandy, clay-like soil. Finding an area to grow crops was difficult. Even though the valleys offered water, they were sometimes too narrow and had a shorter growing season. Many of the nearby streams and rivers would dry up for long periods of time. Many Pueblos were forced to settle around large rivers such as the Rio Grande.

For hundreds of years, the Pueblos existed in this beautiful, but challenging place. The mountains were thought to be holy places, the houses of the supernatural spirits and gods. Waters, such as lakes and springs, were held sacred. The religion of the Pueblos bonded the people with their land in respectful harmony.

CLIFF DWELLERS

The Pueblos were known as the "cliff dwellers." This nickname was derived from the location of their houses and villages which were built along the sides of canyons or cliffs. Some were built as high as five stories, creating the first apartment houses in the United States, or perhaps in the world.

The Pueblo dwellings were often made entirely of earth. Adobe, which is a sandy clay found in Arizona and New Mexico, could be molded and shaped easily when wet. It would not crack or shrink in the extremely hot climate conditions of this desert land. Adobe was therefore used for mortar and plaster in the construction of Pueblo homes.

Roof beams were made from timber. The Indians would travel to the mountains by foot to cut whatever

THESE CLIFF DWELLING ARE NESTLED BENEATH A SHEER ROCK OVERHANG AT THE CANYON DE CHELLY NATIONAL MONUMENT IN ARIZONA.

kinds of wood they could find to bring back. Chopping and shaping the wood was difficult because their available tools were not made for this activity.

In the construction of the pueblos, the men were the masons, or builders, and the women did the plastering. Sometimes the men and women worked together on the entire construction of the pueblo. The women constructed the roof, while the men lifted the heavy beams into place. Friends and relatives helped in constructing the pueblo, accepting meals as payment. Because the meals were such a large expense to the Indians, they tried to employ as few workers as possible.

With religion a strong part of their daily lives, the Pueblos had special prayers and ceremonies to accompany house-building. Before building a house, the man would have prayer feathers prepared by a religious leader to protect the house and the people living in it. Four small eagle feathers would be obtained. To each feather, a small string would be attached. Sacred cornmeal would be sprinkled on the feathers to offer prayers for the house and its occupants.

The man would then take the four feathers and place them on each of the four corners where the house was to be built. Each feather was covered with a large stone, and a mixture of cornmeal and herbs was then sprinkled to form lines between each of the four stones. As the man sprinkled this special mixture, he would chant an ancient housebuilding song. Construction of the house would then begin.

During rainy seasons, storms would be a threat to the adobe walls of the dwellings. Heavy rains or standing water could wear away the masonry and roofs. Special roof drains or spouts were constructed to get water off the roof as soon as possible. A slanted, narrow stone slab was inserted to direct the flow of water. If stone slabs were not available to use as spouts, hollowed-out tree trunks or a curved half of a gourd could be used.

When the walls, roof, and floor were finished, and the outside walls were plastered, another ceremony was performed. Crumbs were sprinkled along the rafters of the house to bring good health to the people living there. A religious leader would then make four more prayer feathers and tie them to the central beam with prayers for the safety of those under the roof.

The early Pueblos homes were often built on the sides of cliffs and mesas, sites difficult to reach, as protection from their enemies. The houses were built close together around a central area called a plaza. Narrow covered passageways allowed the people to move freely through the crowded clusters of houses.

A CLOSEUP VIEW OF THE CLIFF DWELLINGS AT MESA VERDE
NATIONAL PARK IN SOUTHWEST COLORADO.

Few windows or doorways were constructed to aid in the defense of people. Using ladders to enter the buildings also served as protection, for they could be pulled up at any time.

Each Pueblo family lived in a single room. Families living on the upper levels climbed up ladders onto the roof, and down through a hole, or hatch-way, in the roof into their own room.

This one room was the home of the entire family. Because of limited space, the Pueblos learned to make their houses neat and well-organized. Furniture was built-in to save space in the Pueblo dwelling. Ledges were built along opposite sides of the room. The ledges resembled benches, but were actually shelves for storage. A small storage bin for grains and beans would sometimes be added to a corner of the room. A fireplace would be built in another corner of the room for cooking and heating purposes.

A significant part of every Pueblo home was the trough containing *metates*, milling stones used to grind the corn. The trough was built near a corner of the room with space behind it for the woman to kneel while grinding corn. The trough contained three grinding stones separated in different compart-ments. Each grinding stone was about 3-inches (8-cm) thick and sat in a slanted position in its compart-ment. The first stone was made from basalt, or a

(TOP) A VIEW OF THE INTERIOR OF A TYPICAL ONE-ROOM
PUEBLO HOME. (BOTTOM) THIS METATE WAS USED BY
PUEBLO WOMAN TO GRIND THE FAMILY'S CORN.

coarse lava rock. The second stone was made of sandstone, and the third of a fine sandstone. A *manos,* or a cylinder-shaped stone, the width of each grinding stone was used by the women and girls to crush and grind the corn against the grinding stones.

To keep the pueblo uncluttered, storage spaces were designed along the walls. Hanging poles were designed to use as clothing racks and for hanging blankets and robes when they were not being used. Small openings in the walls served as cupboards for storing bowls, food, and small items.

No tables or chairs were to be found, as the family sat on the floor to eat, using rolled blankets as seats. Blankets, rugs, or sheepskins were used to sleep on and hung during the day on the clothes pole.

The Pueblo homes were used mainly for sleeping and protective shelter from threatening weather or enemies. Most of the families' daily activities were outside of the home. The outside terrace areas provided outdoor kitchens and sitting rooms. Basket-weaving and pottery were often worked on outside.

From the first signs of dawn, the family members would begin their day hanging up bedding and washing. Work was done first and eating later. The men would head for the fields, while the women would sweep the floor and begin preparing the day's food. Children would learn by helping, the boys following

THE TROUGH IN THE CORNER OF THIS PUEBLO HOME CONTAINS
THREE SEPARATE GRINDING STONES. EACH STONE PRODUCED A
PROGRESSIVELY FINER GRIND FOR THE CORN.

their fathers and uncles into the fields, and the girls helping their mothers and aunts to grind the corn and collect firewood. The elder members of the tribe would teach younger children how to weave and do pottery.

Rooms not occupied with families were used for storage. Storing and preserving food was essential to the Pueblos' survival. A year or two of stored food was needed in case of a drought. The hot desert sun provided a good means of drying and preserving food. Dark inner rooms of the plaza were used for storage. Corn was neatly stacked in piles according to color and quality. Dried fruits, vegetables, and meats were also stored. Other storage areas were used to keep materials for basket weaving, firewood, and stones needed to make tools and household equipment. After special ceremonies, a prayer feather would be placed in the storage room for extra blessings as the food was stacked away.

Most of the cliff dwellings had watch towers attached to the building or standing nearby. The dwellings could only be entered by ladders. Therefore, the ladders could be pulled up for easy defense against attackers.

Many people have wondered how the Pueblo Indians came to construct their dwellings in this way.

Some think they were built as protection from wild animals or hostile Indian tribes. Because the Indians were continuously adding on new rooms, some archaeologists think they were built as an outlet for energy and aggression, since they did not believe in fighting or wars.

Scientific evidence suggests that these cliff dwellings were abandoned. Some experts believe fierce attacks by nomads caused the Pueblos to leave. A more likely reason, according to tree ring studies, would be the draught caused by insufficient rainfall for nearly twenty years. Scholars believe that many Pueblos traveled southward to make new homes close to the great rivers, such as the Rio Grande.

KIVA: "OLD HOUSE"

In front of the Pueblo villages stood rounded structures whose roofs were flush with the ground. These centers were called *kivas* (kee-vas). The term "kiva" comes from the Hopi, meaning "old house." Kivas were used in much the same way as they are by Pueblo Indians today, as a church or meetinghouse. Each group or clan had its own kiva.

These sacred ceremonial chambers were used by their members to perform secret rites from which other members of the Pueblo village were excluded. Most kivas were built below ground with the opening of the kiva at ground level. These stone rooms had no doors and could only be entered through roof hatchways by a ladder. Walls of some kivas were decorated with murals showing symbols and ceremonies that were important to the Pueblos.

THE LADDER IN THE FOREGROUND LEADS
DOWN INTO A KIVA. THE OLD SECTION OF A
PUEBLO IS IN THE BACKGROUND.

Secret rites of initiation into manhood would take place. Masked dancers would enter the kiva during the ceremony. During this time, young boys entering manhood would discover the masked dancers were really men, not gods.

The occupants of the kiva would chant, invoking deities (spirits) to bring crops. Dances were planned to bring rain, help the hunt, or prepare for spring planting. No white men were allowed to enter the kiva. It was a place for the men to gather together and talk about how to live a spiritual life. Women were allowed to enter the kivas to plaster the walls and for occasional ceremonies.

A sacred cavity, or opening, called the *sipapu* could be found on the floor of the kiva. Spirits or power of the gods would enter through the sipapu.

The Pueblo houses would be built around the kiva to enclose and protect it from outside intruders. From the terraces above, the people of the village would watch masked dancers, called *Kachinas*, emerge from the hatchway of the kiva to perform ceremonial dances in the courtyard. The spectators would sprinkle cornmeal on the dancers as they listened to the songs.

The size of the kiva was determined by the number of men using it and on the types of rituals and ceremonies they would perform. Most kivas were

THE INTERIOR OF AN ANCIENT KIVA

about 25-feet (8-m) long and about 12-feet (4-m) wide. They were built to be between 5-feet (1.5-m) and 8-feet (2.5-m) high.

A hatchway about 5-feet (1.5-m) by 7-feet (2-m) would be constructed in the roof of the kiva for entering and exiting members. The hatchway also served as a vent for smoke and as the only window of the kiva. It was made large enough to allow elaborately dressed dancers to come in and out. A stone slab or tightly woven mat would be used as a cover to close the kiva hatchway when necessary.

Inside the kiva one would find smoothly plastered walls and a floor covered with stone slabs. A special platform was built along one end of the kiva for women and visitors who were invited to witness a ceremony.

Opposite the platform, at the other end of the room, was a low shelf built to display sacred objects. Special ceremonial masks were exhibited in a niche in the wall behind the shelf.

Ledges were built along the side walls for benches in some kivas. A fire pit was made directly below the hatchway. The fire pit was usually about a foot square. Loom attachments were sometimes built in kivas, as many men would use the kivas to do their blanket weaving.

A DETAIL FROM A KIVA MURAL

When the kiva was finally constructed, the clan would perform ceremonies to feed the house, followed by feasting and dancing. It was at this time that the head of the clan would announce the name by which the kiva was to be known.

There may have been several kivas in a pueblo, but only one was considered the main kiva of the village. The most elaborate ceremonies would be held in this kiva. All business, ceremonies, and membership of the kiva were controlled by the clan head. Upon his death, the oldest son of his oldest sister would become the new clan head.

Kivas were also used for learning and great teachings of the elderly men of the tribe.

RELIGION AND CEREMONIES

The arrival of the Spaniards forced a change in religious practices of the Pueblo Indians. The Spanish established churches in all the pueblos. They designed the churches and had the Indians construct them out of adobe bricks. The Indians were forced to haul all the clay for the adobe up the steep cliffs from the valley below to make the Spanish churches.

Even though the Pueblos followed their "new religion" outwardly, they secretly continued to practice their own religious beliefs.

Pueblo religion teaches a oneness with the gods and nature. Pueblo people were taught that there was a spirit-being in all things, such as clouds, trees, animals, corn plants, rain, and mountains. For this reason, everything was honored and used with great

AMONG THE MANY
CEREMONIES HELD
BY THE PUEBLO
INDIANS IS THE CORN
DANCE. THESE
PHOTOS ARE FROM
THE CEREMONY
HELD AT SANTA
CLARA PUEBLO IN
NEW MEXICO.

respect. The Pueblos were a peaceful people—they would pray over an animal they had just slain for food, asking its forgiveness.

The elder men of the tribe were the priests. They would name the proper rituals for planting, getting rain, changing the course of storms, curing illnesses, and defending the village. They ruled the entire village.

One of the highest ideals of the Pueblos was the correct behavior and discipline in carrying out the rituals without mistakes. Each ritual had a special purpose. The Pueblo people made sure just the right costumes were worn, the right chants were sung, and everyone performed their parts flawlessly. Careful planning went into each ritual, as the result they wanted could only be obtained through correct precision of the performance.

The Pueblo Indians feared war gods and worshiped a Mother Earth and Father Sky. Each village had at least one "Kachina" cult, some villages as many as six. They would honor the Kachinas, the supernatural beings who were considered messengers between gods and humans.

In the Pueblo villages, masked dancers played a main part in the tribal ceremonies. These masked dancers were called "Kachinas." Kachina has three meanings: the supernatural being, the dancer dressed in costume impersonating this supernatural being, and a doll made for the children of the tribe to help them learn about their tribe's beliefs.

There were many Kachinas—about 250 have been counted. Each one has a particular name and is connected with a myth. The Kachinas visited the villages during the first half of each year to dance and sing and bring gifts to the children. Their arrival and ceremonies were thought to bring rain to help the crops grow. The Kachinas represented friendly spirits, although several were to be feared, as they punished those members of the tribe who did not abide by the ceremonial and social laws of the village.

In each village, every man belonged to at least one Kachina cult. Boys were initiated at about twelve years of age. Children were led to believe that the human Kachina dancers were the real Kachinas.

Kachina dancers were always men, even though they sometimes represented female spirits. When a Pueblo man would put on a mask to dance, it is said that he would lose his own identity and actually become the Kachina that he represented. Women would take part in many sacred dances, but would never wear masks.

Women could also belong to a Kachina cult. There were two ways this could happen. First, if a woman was cured by a Kachina cult ritual, she had to

THIS BUFFALO DANCE, HELD ON CHRISTMAS DAY IN SAN
ILDEFONSO PUEBLO, NEW MEXICO, CELEBRATES THE CLOSE AND
SPECIAL RELATIONSHIP BETWEEN THE PUEBLOS AND ANIMALS.

(TOP) THE DEER DANCE
HELD AT SAN JUAN
PUEBLO IN NEW MEXICO.
(RIGHT) THIS YOUNG BOY
IS PARTICIPATING IN THE
COMANCHE DANCE AT
SAN JUAN PUEBLO.
TRADITIONAL BELIEFS
ARE PASSED FROM
GENERATION TO
GENERATION THROUGH
THE PUEBLO DANCES
AND RITUALS.

join. Secondly, if a woman mistakenly entered a kiva while a ceremony was going on, membership would also be required. Members of the Kachina cult were responsible for making masks, Kachina dolls for the little girls, and conducting Kachina dances.

Kachina dolls, fruits, miniature bows and arrows, and other gifts would be given to the children of the village by certain Kachina dancers. The Kachina dolls were not given as toys, but to help the children become familiar with the spirits that are important to their religion.

Sacred clowns, called "mudheads" were an integral part of many ceremonies. The clowns would perform between the more serious ceremonies. Their foolish acts and dances would bring laughter to the people. In some villages, the clowns would make fun of people in the village to remind them of their shortcomings and help them to better themselves.

Eagle, Buffalo and Deer Dances were done in the Rio Grande Pueblos. The purpose of these dances was to show the relationship between man and animals. The Rain, Corn, and Harvest Dances also played an important role in their ritual life, especially because the Pueblos were traditionally farmers.

Small children were encouraged to participate in most Pueblo dances. This is so traditions would be taught at a young age to small children.

THE LAND AND FARMING

The area of land inhabited by the Pueblo people was not a desirable place to live. It had a hot climate and an annual rainfall of less than 20 inches (51 cm). Because of its climate, much of the land is desert or semidesert. It was also bordered with mountain ranges and flat mesas rising from level plateaus. Farming Indians of the southwest, such as the Pueblos, had to use keen observation and judgment in chosing the locations for their farms.

Gentle sloping rocks or valley floors usually provided a good location for growing crops. Small dams were built to control the flow of water to the crops. Dams were sometimes structured around separate plants to protect them from summer flood waters.

CORN IS AN IMPORTANT CROP TO THE PUEBLO INDIANS
FOR BOTH FOOD AND RITUAL.

Another farming practice was dry farming, which means taking advantage of the little rain that falls by planting crops in certain ways. Digging irrigation canals and ditches to bring water to crops from nearby streams or rivers was a method used during times of little rainfall.

Corn was the most important crop. Along with corn, the Pueblos grew squash, pumpkins, melons, and beans. The Pueblos did not plow. They would leave the crusty cover of the earth untouched to protect the dampness underneath. Seeds were planted deep so that roots could reach the dampness. At one time, Pueblo farmers used wooden tools, but as years went on, they learned to use tools introduced by Europeans.

Families would sometimes camp in the fields during the farming season. Temporary housing structures were built for them to live in during this time. When the planting and harvesting were completed, the families would return to their main pueblo.

RESPONSIBILITIES OF TRIBE MEMBERS

The Pueblo Woman ➤ Women played an important role in the Pueblo village. In many pueblos, the house belonged to the man's wife. The Pueblo men were careful not to marry outside their own villages and not to marry a close relative.

Pueblo women dressed alike, wearing cotton house dresses with shawls over their heads. Special costumes were worn for their dances. Their hair was twisted in a tight knot at the nape of the neck, with bangs adorning the forehead. For certain ceremonial dances, the women would let their hair flow loosely down their backs without the shawl.

Women wore either high moccasins, or low moccasins. The high moccasins were made of deerskin and sometimes folded down below their knees. The folds served as pockets for tools or weapons.

(TOP) THIS 1935 PHOTOGRAPH SHOWS A WOMAN GRINDING CORN AT SAN JUAN PUEBLO. (BOTTOM) BREAD IS BAKED IN SANTA CLARA PUEBLO TODAY MUCH AS IT HAS BEEN FOR CENTURIES.

Pueblo women seldom carried their babies on their back. They did not use cradle boards. This was because they did not work in the fields like some Indian women. The responsibilities of the Pueblo women were to cook, bake, clean, and care for the children. They would also carry water from the rivers or streams. Instead of cleaning their houses thoroughly each spring and fall, they would newly plaster the walls, inside and out. The women were also the pottery makers of the tribe.

The Pueblo Man ➤ The Pueblo man would use a cotton sheet blanket as part of his dress. When the weather was cold, it was used as a shawl, and in hot weather it was wrapped around the waist like a sash. Moccasins were also worn when working around the pueblos, fishing, hunting, or farming.

The men did not shave. They would pull their facial hairs out one by one. After doing this for some time, the hair practically stopped growing. Many of the older men also pulled out their eyelashes.

Most of the Pueblo men were farmers. They had to irrigate the fields, taking turns to clean out the ditches. When the land wore out, they would have to change their crops and raise fewer sheep. The men were the hunters of the village, as well as the caretakers of the animals. Along with these many jobs of the Pueblo man was the responsibility of the weaving.

THE ARID, HARSH CLIMATE OF NEW MEXICO DEMANDS THAT MUCH ATTENTION BE GIVEN TO CROPS SUCH AS CORN.

YOUNG GIRLS SHARE A PRIVATE MOMENT DURING A
FESTIVAL DAY AT SANTA CLARA PUEBLO.

The Pueblo Children ➝ The children of the Pueblos shared in the responsibilities of the village. Girls were taught by their mothers the art of cooking, pottery making, cleaning, and caring for the younger children. The Pueblo boys were taught at a young age by their fathers to farm as well as the methods of irrigation, hunting, and weaving.

For entertainment, the children had games they would play. Two of these games were called Shinny and Playhouse. Shinny was played with a curved stick and ball made out of stuffed deerskin. The boys would run fast and drive the ball with the stick, but did not try to reach a goal. Playhouse was a game enjoyed by the little girls. Dolls made of wood or cornhusks were made and used to play this game.

MODERN PUEBLOS

About thirty Pueblo villages are inhabited today. The Pueblo Indians have had to learn to live in a white man's world. Most Pueblos have been able to adapt to new living conditions and still maintain their own cultural and traditional values.

Modern Pueblo Indians still live in houses similar to their ancestors'. Doors on the ground floor are used for entering and exiting instead of hatchways. Larger window areas with glass have replaced the small window openings. Pyramid-shaped roofs are built instead of the traditional flat roof. Most Pueblo homes today have two or more rooms for one family. Their homes have also been remodeled to include conveniences such as kitchens and bathrooms.

LAGUNA PUEBLO, NEW MEXICO

Most Pueblos homes today rarely have more than two stories.

The covered passages connecting the plazas are now open. Most Pueblos have electricity, running water, and bottled gas.

Today, Pueblo families build their homes close to their crops and water sites. Some of the people live in houses outside of the village, but return to the old village for special council meetings and ceremonies.

Many Pueblos have entered the "cash" economy of the United States. Their way of living may be the practicing and selling of crafts they are so well-known for, such as the weaving of "mantas," the traditional woman's dress, or dance kilts and rain sashes. These clothing items are still used in ceremonial dances. Pottery, silverware, and jewelry made of silver, turquoise, shell, and coral are also marketable.

Many Pueblos with college educations are active in Indian education and administration, or in the fields of medicine, health work, or the arts.

In the past, the Pueblo Indians' way of life rarely changed. Families were close-knit, and people put their energies into family and community life. They were peaceful people and fought only when attacked. They did not honor any warriors or people who wanted to compete with fellow tribe members for prestige.

THIS SANTA ANA POTTER DISPLAYS SOME OF HER
BEAUTIFUL CRAFT WORK.

Today's Pueblos hold onto and pass down to
their children these core values and beliefs, regardless
of the forever changing world around them.

GLOSSARY

Adobe clay from the ground from which sun-dried brick is made.

Anthropologist a person who studies mankind's physical and cultural characteristics, customs, and social relationships.

Archaeologist a person who studies ancient civilizations by digging up artifacts and relics.

Basalt a dark, tough volcanic rock.

Cult a system of religious worship or ritual.

Kilt a skirt.

Mesa a small, high plateau.

Mission headquarters, or place where people lived or worked.

Mural   a picture painted directly on a wall.

Niche   a hollow place in a wall that can be used for storage.

Plaza   a public area in a city or village.

Pueblo   a communal village consisting of one or more flat-roofed structures of stone or adobe that were arranged in terraces and housed a number of people.

Rite   a ceremonial procedure.

Ritual   a set system or format of rites.

Sacred   regarded with respect and reverence.

Sagebrush   a plant found in dry areas of the United States.

Sash   a decorated band, ribbon, or scarf worn over the shoulder or around the waist.

Spirit   a supernatural being believed to inhabit a certain region and can represent good or evil.

Supernatural   something believed to exist or occur outside the normal knowledge of humans.

Terrace   a raised, flat mound of earth with sloping sides.

Turquoise   a semiprecious stone, usually of a greenish-blue color.

FOR FURTHER READING

Avery, Susan and Linda Skinner. *Extraordinary American Indians*. Chicago: Childrens Press, 1992.

Bahti, Tom. *Southwestern Indian Ceremonials*. Flagstaff, Ariz.:KC Publications, 1970.

Bahti, Tom. *Southwestern Indian Tribes*. Flagstaff, Ariz.: KC Publications, 1968.

Clark, Ann Nolan. *Circle of Seasons*. New York: Farrar, 1970.

D'Apice. *Pueblo*. Vero Beach, Florida: Rourke Corp., 1990.

Hallet, Bill and Jane Hallett. *Pueblo Indians of New Mexico: Activities & Adventures for Kids*. Tucson, Ariz.: Look & See, 1992.

Ortiz, Alfonso. *Pueblo*. New York: Chelsea House, 1992.

Yue, Charlotte. *Pueblo*. New York: Houghton Mifflin, 1986.

INDEX

ABOUT THE AUTHOR

Suzanne Powell resides in Grand Rapids, Michigan, with her family. She is an elementary teacher and has a special interest in studying the cultural background of the North American Indian tribes. Her study of the Pueblo Indians was sparked from a trip to New Mexico during which she was involved in art classes from American Indian instructors. At that time, trips to museums, reservations, and the cliff-dwellings were part of her learning experience.

Powell is co-author, with Patricia Ryon Quiri, of *Stranger Danger*, published in 1985.